Our WILD™ WORLD SERIES

Sharks

Laura Evert
Illustrations by John F. McGee

NorthWord Press
Minnetonka, Minnesota

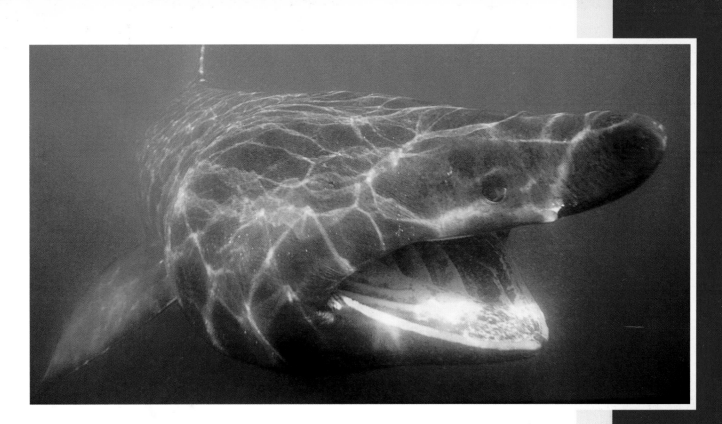

ARE YOU AFRAID OF SHARKS? Many people are. They think that all sharks are dangerous "killers," swimming near beaches in search of their next meal. In fact, very few sharks are a threat to humans, and in those cases, attacks are usually due to mistaken identity. The truth is that all sharks are fascinating animals that deserve not only our respect, but also our understanding.

Sharks have been around for more than 400 million years, and unlike other animals, they have not changed very much in that time. There are over 380 different species (SPEE-sees), or kinds, of sharks throughout the world. About 115 species live near North America. At least one species can be found in every ocean. The Greenland shark, for example, can be found swimming in the waters of the Arctic Ocean, while huge basking sharks can be found at the opposite end of the world, near Antarctica.

Great white sharks can be found in many oceans of the world, especially near the coast, where they hunt for seals.

The slow-swimming basking shark is usually gray-brown, but it may be black.

Sharks come in all shapes and sizes. They often get their name from the way they look, or how they behave. Some, like the pygmy shark, are so small that they can fit in your hand. The pygmy shark measures only about 6 inches (15 centimeters) long. The whale shark is the biggest shark. It can grow to be over 50 feet (15 meters) long! Some sharks are thin, like the blue shark. Some are fat, like the bull shark. And some are just plain strange-looking, like the hammerhead with its wide, flat head and one eye on each edge.

The cookie cutter shark gets its name from the way it eats. When open, its mouth forms a circle of sharp teeth. It attaches to another fish or sea mammal with its mouth, twists its entire body and cuts out a perfectly round piece of flesh for dinner. The goblin shark has a long, pointed snout with a beak-like mouth underneath. Its front teeth are like needles, and it has a flabby, pink-gray body. The goblin shark is very rare and secretive, so not many have been seen.

No matter what they look like or how they behave, all sharks have one thing in common. They are all fish. That means they breathe with gills instead of lungs like mammals do.

Sharks
FUNFACT:

Basking sharks may swim in large groups of up to 100 while scooping up plankton and krill. But most sharks prefer to hunt alone, and do not like the company of other sharks.

Groups of gray reef sharks sometimes surprise a school of fish from below and force them to the surface, where they cannot escape.

The nurse shark can create enough suction with its thick mouth to suck food out from between rocks. It is a night hunter that rests during the day.

Sharks have 5 to 7 gill slits, or openings, on each side of their body, just behind the head. Most sharks get the oxygen they need by taking in water through the mouth, passing it over the gills, then sending it out through the gill slits. As the water passes over the gills, the oxygen in the seawater is absorbed and transferred to the shark's bloodstream. Many sharks must swim almost constantly to keep water flowing into their mouth.

Other sharks, like the nurse shark, spend almost all their time on the ocean floor. They breathe in a way that doesn't require them to be in motion. Behind each eye these sharks have a tiny opening, called a spiracle (SPEER-uh-cul), that sucks in water and pumps it over the gills and out through the gill slits. Because the spiracles are located on the top of their heads the sharks breathe in clean water from above, instead of the mucky water they stir up as they move along the bottom of the sea searching for food. These kinds of sharks are called bottom dwellers.

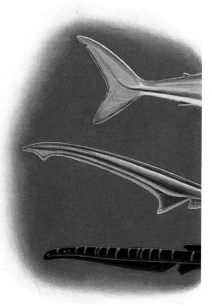

Great White Shark

Thresher Shark

Zebra Shark

Like other fish, sharks have fins. In fact, sharks have five different kinds of fins. They have two pectoral (pek-TOR-ul) fins, one on each side of the lower front part of the body. They lift the shark as it swims. Some species, like blue sharks, have very long pectoral fins. Some, like soupfin sharks, have short pectorals.

The dorsal (DOR-sul) fin on the shark's back helps it balance as it swims through the water. Some sharks, like the bull shark, have a second dorsal fin located just before the tail begins. A dorsal fin breaking through the surface of the water as the shark swims is a sight that alerts people everywhere to the presence of a shark!

A pair of pelvic (PEL-vik) fins located under the body toward the tail also help the shark with balance. They keep the shark from rolling side to side. Some sharks—especially those that need extra balance, like the silky shark—have anal (A-nul) fins even farther toward the tail.

Last, but perhaps most important, sharks have a caudal (KAW-dul) fin that is really part of the tail. The caudal fin has two lobes, or parts. The shark's speed depends on the size of the lobes. If the upper and lower lobes are about the same size, the shark is a very fast swimmer, like the great white shark. That's because a matched pair of lobes gives the shark more power as the tail pushes against the water.

The great white has strong pectoral fins to help it move its large body through the water. Like all sharks, however, it can only swim forward.

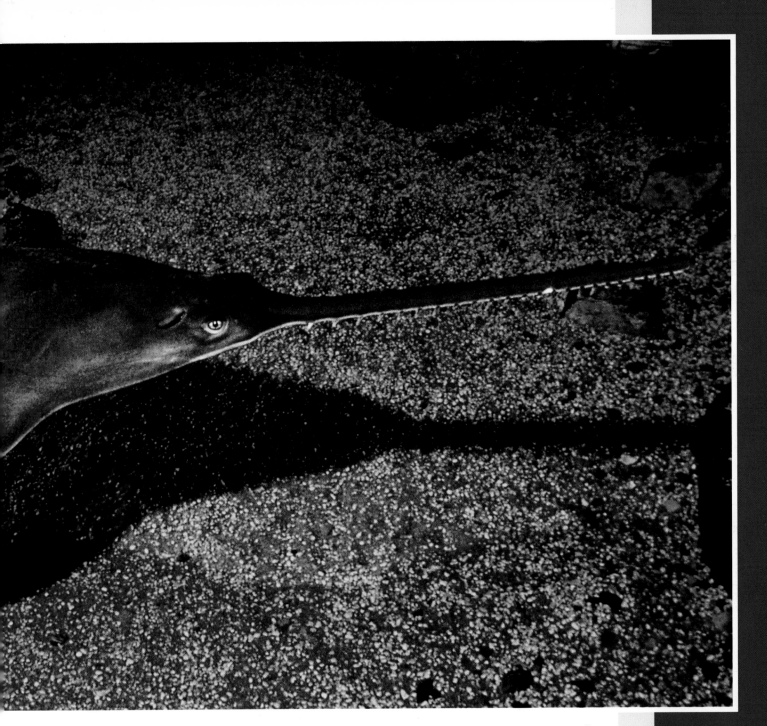

Sawfish sharks usually live in very muddy water, so they cannot see well.
They rely on their long, sensitive snouts for locating food.

Young zebra sharks begin their lives with zebra-like stripes. But the stripes change to leopard-like markings when the sharks become adults.

Some sharks can swim with bursts of speed up to 30 miles (48 kilometers) per hour. Their usual swim rate, however, is more like 1 to 5 miles (1.6 to 8 kilometers) per hour. Different species swim different distances when following or searching for food. The soupfin shark, for example, may travel 35 miles (56 kilometers) in a day.

With tails that have smaller lower lobes, sharks such as the thresher shark are able to twist and turn very quickly while swimming. This helps them catch other fish to eat. The thresher shark also swings its tail from side to side, churning up the water and stunning its food.

Sharks that have almost no lower lobe are not fast swimmers. They are usually bottom dwellers, like nurse and zebra sharks.

The angel shark sometimes hunts for its food by burying itself in the sand and ambushing fish as they swim by.

Body shape also tells us how a particular species of shark lives.

If a shark's body looks flat, it is probably a bottom dweller, like a wobbegong or angel shark. These sharks hug the ocean floor as they move slowly along, searching for shellfish and flatfish like flounder, which blend in with the sand.

If a shark is shaped like a bullet or torpedo, it is designed for speed. With this shape sharks meet less resistance as they shoot through the water with ease. They create very little current and leave almost no wake, or ripple, behind them.

Airplane and submarine engineers have studied the shark's body to see what elements they could copy into their designs!

Besides gills and fins there are not many other similarities shared by sharks and other fish. For one thing, fish don't have to spend much effort to keep from sinking in the water. They have a swim bladder inside their body that fills with air. This helps them remain buoyant (BOY-ant), or able to float. Sharks don't have swim bladders. But they do have a very large liver that is rich with oil. Since oil is lighter than water, it helps to keep the shark from sinking. A shark's liver can weigh hundreds of pounds.

Another difference between sharks and fish is their bones. Fish have stiff bones that don't bend easily. But a shark's bones are made of cartilage, the same flexible material that we have between our bones and in our ears. This flexible cartilage enables sharks to turn quickly while swimming and swing around in different directions.

Sharks
FUNFACT:

Most sharks are cold blooded. Some of the faster, more aggressive sharks like great whites have warmer blood to keep their muscles warm.

By looking at the dorsal fin, it's easy to see how the whitetip reef shark got its name. Its favorite food is octopus.

The tiger shark has tiger-like markings on a dark back with an off-white belly.
Tiger sharks are solitary animals except during mating.

Sharks have many body characteristics that are unique to predators. A predator (PRED-uh-tor) is an animal that hunts other animals for food. The animals it eats are called prey (PRAY). All sharks are carnivores (KAR-nuh-vorz), or meat eaters, and most of them feed on other kinds of fish. Tuna, salmon, squid, and herring are favorite meals for many sharks. Some sharks also eat sea turtles, seals, sea lions, dolphins, octopuses, and even other sharks! Sharks that eat these large prey animals are fast and powerful, like great white, mako, tiger, blue, and bull sharks.

These are also the sharks that are mostly responsible for attacks on swimmers. But that doesn't mean that sharks hunt people as prey. Scientists who study sharks are called elasmobranchologists (ee-laz-mo-bran-KOL-uh-jists). They believe that when a shark bites a human it is probably doing so because it has confused that person with a prey animal, like a sea lion. In most of these cases of mistaken identity, the shark leaves as soon as it realizes its error.

And just because a person is in the water while a shark swims nearby does not necessarily mean the shark is going to bite. Sharks only feed when they are hungry. If their last meal was a hearty one, they can wait as long as a month without eating again.

Sharks
FUNFACT:

The sawfish is a shark with a long snout that looks like the toothed blade of a chainsaw. It swishes its head back and forth to strike and stun its prey.

Tiger sharks seem to eat more than any other shark. In fact, they probably could be called the "garbage collectors" of the sea. They have huge appetites and eat almost anything. Scientists have found license plates, tires, shoes, plastic bottles, tin cans, and even pieces of boat oars in their stomachs. Whatever the shark cannot fully digest is eventually brought back up from the stomach and spit out.

Bull sharks are another species that will eat almost anything. Some people consider bull sharks the most dangerous sharks because many live in the same shallow waters near areas where people live. That means these sharks and people have to share the same space.

Bull sharks are also one of a few species that can survive in the fresh water of rivers as well as saltwater oceans. In late April through July, bull sharks may be found at the mouth of the Mississippi River while giving birth to their babies. They also have been found as far as 2,000 miles (3,218 kilometers) up the Amazon River.

Sharks
FUNFACT:

We can determine a shark's age by counting the growth rings of its vertebrae, or backbones. It's like counting tree rings. Some sharks live to be 25 years old, and some may live to be over 150!

Bull sharks eat mostly fish, but they will eat almost anything, including other sharks, rays, and turtles.

Blue sharks are easy to identify by their pointed snout and very large eyes.
Their slender body is dark to light shades of blue, and the belly is white.

Most sharks that hunt prey do so at night. That may sound difficult, but sharks have keen hunting senses.

In the back of each eye, sharks have a tapetum (tuh-PEE-tum). It helps reflect light back into the eye, like a little mirror. Many land animals that have good night vision, like cats and dogs, also have tapetums.

Scientists also think that sharks can see in color and up to seven times better than we can.

A shark has taste buds in its mouth, but not on its tongue, as humans do. When it bites into something, it can tell if it's the right kind of food.

But most researchers think that a shark's sense of taste is not very important because it usually just swallows its prey whole.

The silvertip can be a curious shark and will often come to the surface to see what is going on. It often swims very close to divers.

A shark's ears are inside its head. A tube from each inner ear is connected to two little holes on the outside of the skin. Sound moves through the water in the form of vibrations. The ears receive the vibrations through the tubes and send messages to the shark's brain. This is usually the first sense that alerts the shark to investigate something that could be prey. We don't know exactly how well sharks hear, but researchers think they can hear sounds about 300 yards (274 meters) away. That's about as long as three football fields!

The sense of touch for all fish, including sharks, is different than it is for humans. We feel things through nerve endings all over our bodies and in our fingertips, but sharks don't often actually touch objects.

As something moves in the water it creates vibrations. The water carries those movement vibrations through holes in the shark's skin into tiny tubes that make up a sense called the lateral line. As the vibrations come in contact with many little nerve endings in the lateral line, the shark learns what its favorite prey's swimming pattern "feels" like. It is one of the senses that makes hunting more successful for sharks.

As a shark moves through the sea, water flows into its nostrils, which are located on either side of its snout. This is how the shark smells. To pinpoint where a scent (SENT), or odor, is coming from, the shark turns in the direction of the smell and swims toward it. Occasionally it swings its snout from side to side, to make sure it is still on track. The shark usually does not stop until it has found and identified the smell.

These five senses are similar to those of humans and other animals. But sharks have a sixth sense that others don't have.

Lateral Line

If food is plentiful, some sharks, like this Caribbean reef shark, may live in the same small area for as long as two years.

Every living thing gives off some sort of electrical impulse. Even if you are perfectly motionless the beating of your heart sends out an impulse. Sharks can detect even the faintest electrical impulses in the water by using their ampullae of Lorenzini (am-PEW-lie of lor-en-ZEE-nee). The ampullae are tiny capsules connected by tubes to openings in the shark's skin, scattered over the shark's snout. The capsules are filled with a jelly-like material that receives electric impulses in the water and sends messages to the shark's brain. No creature can escape the detection of a shark once its impulse has been picked up by the ampullae.

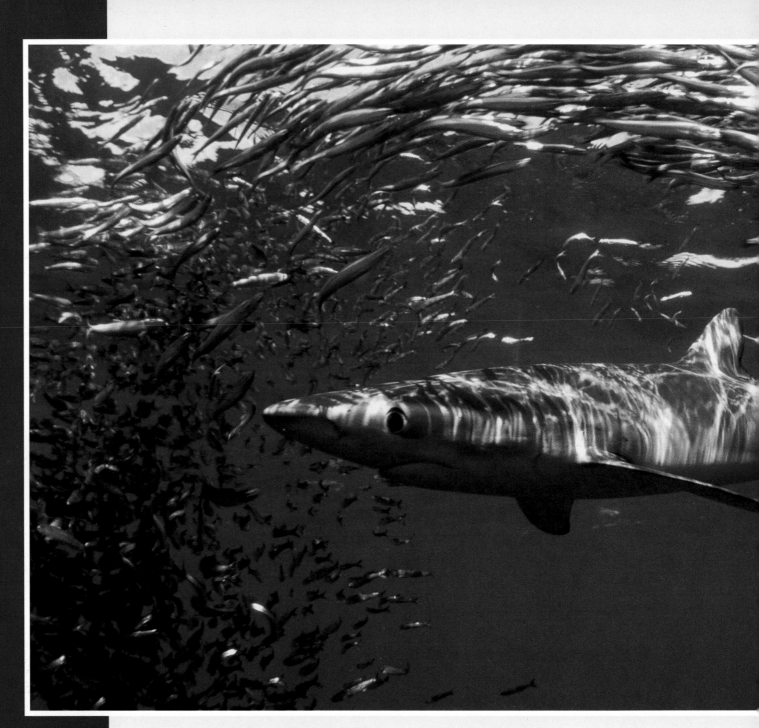

There are probably more blue sharks throughout the world's oceans than any other species of shark.

All of a shark's senses work together, one after another, to help it locate and identify potential prey. First, the shark hears the sound with its inner ears. Next, it smells the scent. Then it feels the prey's motion vibrations with its lateral line, sees the prey with its eyes, and zeros in on the identity and location of the prey with the ampullae.

Imagine, then, how confusing it must be to a shark to be near a beach with people shouting, splashing, diving, and swimming. It's no wonder that some sharks swim up to the beach out of simple curiosity!

The markings of a whale shark make it easy to identify,
even with its huge mouth closed.

Whale sharks are not ready to mate until they are about 30 years old.
Scientists think they may live up to 150 years.

You might think that the biggest sharks are the ones that are the most dangerous. Actually, just the opposite is true. Whale sharks are really gentle, although it is easy to understand why some people might be afraid of them because of their enormous size. The whale shark is the largest fish in the ocean. It can grow to be over 50 feet (15 meters) long. It would be difficult to weigh such a large fish, but scientists think that one so big would probably weigh about 9 tons (8 metric tons). That's about as long as one school bus and the weight of two combined!

These huge creatures swim quietly through the sea with their mouth opened wide. It's like a vacuum cleaner. Every small thing in their path is sucked in. They feed on schools of tiny fish, such as anchovies, and microscopic plants and animals called plankton. Water that is scooped in along with the food is filtered out by gill rakers as it passes through the gill slits.

Because whale sharks have a very narrow throat, they usually eat only what they can swallow whole, like small fish. Whale sharks do have teeth, but they are used only to keep the food from escaping back out of the mouth before swallowing. The 3,000 teeth are as tiny as a person's baby teeth!

Sharks
FUNFACT:

Some small sharks that live in deep water give off a glowing light from their bodies. Scientists think this may attract prey or help the sharks see each other.

Each species of shark has different shapes and sizes of teeth. But one thing that they all have in common is that no matter how many teeth break or fall out, there is an endless supply of new teeth waiting to fill the gap. The teeth grow in rows. Sharks can use just one row or several rows at a time. The rows simply rise up or lower depending on how much biting force the shark needs.

When one tooth falls out or breaks off, the tooth behind it in the row moves forward to take its place. New teeth are stored in the shark's jaw until they are needed. Then they push forward. Sometimes a shark may lose and replace an entire row of teeth at one time. Elasmobranchologists think that a shark may replace up to 30,000 teeth during its lifetime.

Some teeth look like long, thin, smooth daggers. These teeth are best for sharks like makos that grab their prey with a stabbing motion and quickly swallow it whole. Some teeth are wide, with pointed tips.

Bull and tiger sharks have this kind of teeth because they must be able to hold onto the larger prey they catch. Their teeth also have sharp jagged edges, or serrations (sare-A-shuns), along the sides—like a steak knife. If the food is too big to be swallowed whole, the serrations cut it into chunks.

Most bottom dwellers have short, stubby teeth with several points. These teeth are helpful for cracking and crushing the shells of lobsters, crabs, and other shellfish that move along the ocean floor.

Another thing that sets sharks apart from other fish is how their jaws work. Most fish, like most other animals, have hinged jaws that open only as wide as their mouth allows. Sharks have separate upper and lower jaws. They are free-floating in the shark's mouth, held together only by muscles. This means sharks can open their mouth as wide as their head! Great whites, for example, can open their mouth almost 4 feet (1.2 meters) wide. And if that isn't amazing enough, they can also push their jaws outside their mouth for maximum bite.

Sharks
FUNFACT:

Over time, some sharks have been given nicknames. The zebra shark, for instance, is also known as the monkey-mouthed shark.

Great white sharks are called apex predators. This means that they eat anything they want and nothing eats them.

The only place you probably expect to find teeth on a shark is in its mouth. Surprise! The skin of a shark is covered from snout to tail with a layer of denticles (DEN-ti-kuls), which means "tiny teeth." Denticles are made of the same material as teeth. Most sharks have denticles that overlap each other in a continuous pattern, like shingles on a house. If you could move your hand along a shark's skin starting at the nose and going toward the tail, it would feel smooth. If you went from the tail toward the head, you would be in for an unpleasant surprise. Depending on the shark, the skin would feel rough like sandpaper or sharp like a cheese grater.

You probably know that leopards have spots, zebras have stripes, and lots of other animals have markings on their bodies for camouflage (KAM-uh-flaj). Camouflage helps animals blend into their surroundings so they are hidden from their predators and their prey.

Most sharks have a kind of camouflage called counter shading. This means that they are darker on top and lighter underneath. This shading makes them more difficult to see from above because they blend in with the dark water or ocean floor. And from below, they are lost in the light at the water's surface.

Some sharks that live on the ocean floor have markings, like the chain cat shark's stripes, to help them blend in with the rocks and sand. The wobbegong shark also has flaps of skin around its mouth to help it blend in with seaweed and other plants.

The banded wobbegong lies on the ocean bottom, near coral reefs, waiting for fish to approach. Then it bites its prey with its short but razor-sharp teeth.

These adult nurse sharks are smooth to the touch. They no longer have spots, as they did when they were young.

Sharks may also have scars on their body, especially around the fins. Sharks with wounds such as these are probably females, and they got the scars while mating. Not much is known about the mating behavior of many sharks, especially the larger ones, because they are very secretive during this time. But there are several things we know for sure. When a female shark is ready to mate, she gives off a scent that attracts male sharks. Sometimes one male shark responds to her scent, and sometimes she attracts many males that compete to mate with her.

Before mating begins, the male nips and bites the female, probably to keep her from swimming away. Luckily for the female, she has thicker skin than the male. In some species, like the blue shark, the female's skin is up to twice as thick as the male's. Sometimes the male bites into the female and hangs onto her with his teeth to keep their bodies together while mating. The cuts and bites may hurt the female a little, but they usually do not cause serious wounds.

After mating, baby sharks, called pups, can develop in one of three ways, depending on the species of shark. Some kinds of sharks produce egg cases to protect the developing eggs, or embryos (EM-bree-ohs), inside. The cases are like the shell of a chicken's egg, but they are thicker and tougher, like leather. Some species have egg cases that look like spiral shells. Others' look like little pouches and are sometimes called a "mermaid's purse."

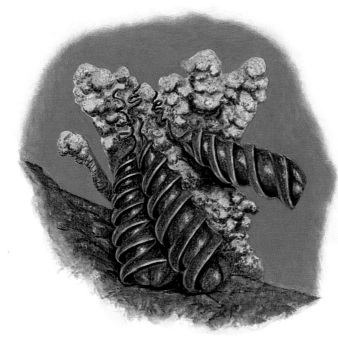

This swell shark pup is ready to survive on its own
as it emerges from its mermaid's purse.

In addition to its interesting stripes, the Port Jackson shark has a small spike on each of the dorsal fins.

Most sharks keep the egg cases inside their body while the embryos grow. After the pups hatch out of the case they live inside their mother for about 10 months to grow a little bigger.

Great white, tiger, and thresher sharks are just a few that have their pups this way. When shark pups are born, they look exactly like tiny versions of adult sharks.

Other sharks, like Port Jackson and swell sharks, deposit the egg cases on the ocean floor, and leave the babies to develop and hatch on their own.

This is a dangerous time for the embryos. Other fish may try to eat them.

Well known for their curiousity, whitetip reef sharks will swim very close to anyone or anything that happens to be in their territory.

These sharks can take up to 15 months to hatch, and then they swim directly into the ocean without any protection.

Some sharks don't make egg cases at all. Their pups grow inside the mother until they are ready to be born. Blue sharks, hammerheads, and some reef sharks have their babies this way. The pups are born tail-first after about 12 months, and they are about 2 feet (60 centimeters) long. After they're born they swim away from their mother and are on their own. The babies quickly swim to shallow water, where they can hide from predators among rocks and plants.

Hammerheads seem to prefer eating stingrays. They kill a ray by using their "hammer" to hold it down while taking bites.

Sharks usually have 4 to 16 pups at a time. But some, like tiger sharks, may have over 50 pups! Although that may sound like a lot of sharks, the truth is that not very many survive.

In fact, sharks all around the world are having difficulty surviving. Hundreds of thousands of sharks are being killed each year for sport and food. Sometimes their fins are used for soup and the rest of the animal is thrown away. Their teeth are used for necklaces and their skin is used for bags and boots. Some people don't understand shark behavior, and kill sharks out of fear.

But sharks play a very important role in the sea. Without them, their prey would multiply so much that they would run out of food. Then *their* prey would multiply and run out of food. The chain reaction could continue and upset the delicate balance of life in the oceans.

Fortunately, many people are working hard to learn more about sharks. And through their studies, we will find new ways to protect and preserve sharks and the precious ocean habitat we share with them.

Sharks
FUNFACT:

Newborn dogfish pups are only about 8 to 12 inches (20 to 30 centimeters) long, and these sharks take over 2 years to develop before they are born.

Internet Sites

You can find out more interesting information about sharks and lots of other wildlife by visiting these web sites.

http://endangered.fws.gov/kids/index.html	U.S. Fish and Wildlife Service
www.animal.discovery.com	Discovery Channel Online
www.cetacea.org/index.htm	Whale and Dolphin Conservation Society
www.EnchantedLearning.com/subjects/sharks	Disney Online
www.kidsgowild.com	Wildlife Conservation Society
www.kidsplanet.org	Defenders of Wildlife
www.nationalgeographic.com/kids	National Geographic Society
www.nwf.org/kids	National Wildlife Federation
www.seaworld.org/infobook.html	Sea World Animal Information Database
www.tnc.org	The Nature Conservancy
www.worldwildlife.org	World Wildlife Fund

Index

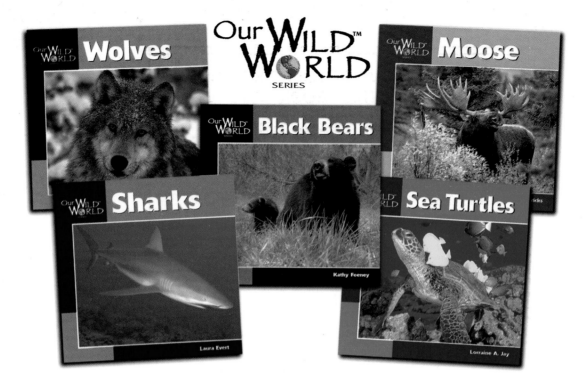

Titles available in the Our Wild World Series:

BISON
ISBN 1-55971-775-0

BLACK BEARS
ISBN 1-55971-742-4

DOLPHINS
ISBN 1-55971-776-9

EAGLES
ISBN 1-55971-777-7

MANATEES
ISBN 1-55971-778-5

MOOSE
ISBN 1-55971-744-0

SEA TURTLES
ISBN 1-55971-746-7

SHARKS
ISBN 1-55971-779-3

WHALES
ISBN 1-55971-780-7

WHITETAIL DEER
ISBN 1-55971-743-2

WOLVES
ISBN 1-55971-748-3

See your nearest bookseller, or order by phone 1-800-328-3895

NORTHWORD PRESS
Minnetonka, Minnesota